The Ultimate Self-Teaching Method!

BEGINNER'S PACK

Play Flute Today!

A Complete Guide to the Basics

PLAYBACK+

Speed • Pitch • Balance • Loop

To access audio and video visit:
www.halleonard.com/mylibrary

Enter Code
5607-4583-7653-0115

ISBN 978-1-5400-5240-7

Visit Hal Leonard Online at
www.halleonard.com

Contact us:
Hal Leonard
7777 West Bluemound Road
Milwaukee, WI 53213
Email: info@halleonard.com

In Europe, contact:
Hal Leonard Europe Limited
42 Wigmore Street
Marylebone, London, W1U 2RN
Email: info@halleonardeurope.com

In Australia, contact:
Hal Leonard Australia Pty. Ltd.
4 Lentara Court
Cheltenham, Victoria, 3192 Australia
Email: info@halleonard.com.au

Introduction

Welcome to *Play Flute Today!*—the series designed to prepare you for any style of flute playing, from rock to blues to jazz to classical. Whatever your taste in music, *Play Flute Today!* will give you the start you need.

About the Audio & Video

It's easy and fun to play flute, and the accompanying audio will make your learning even more enjoyable, as we take you step by step through each lesson and play each song along with a full band. Much as a real lesson, the best way to learn this material is to read and practice a while first on your own, then listen to the audio. With *Play Flute Today!*, you can learn at your own pace. If there is ever something that you don't quite understand the first time through, go back to the track and listen again. Every musical track has been given a track number, so if you want to practice a song again, you can find it right away.

Some topics in the book include video lessons, so you can see and hear the material being taught. Audio and video are indicated with icons.

🔊 Audio Icon   ▶ Video Icon

Contents

The Basics

The Parts of the Flute ▶

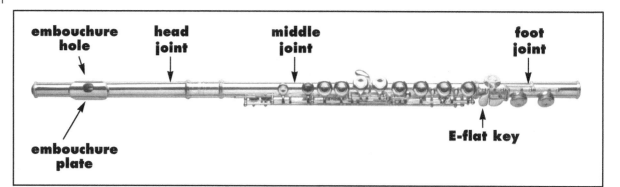

Posture ▶

Whether sitting on the edge of your chair or standing, you should always keep your:

- Spine straight and tall,
- Shoulders back and relaxed, and
- Feet flat on the floor.

Breathing & Air Stream ▶

Breathing is a natural thing we all do constantly, but you must control your breathing while playing the flute. To discover the correct air stream to play your flute:

- Hold your finger about eight inches in front of you.
- Inhale deeply, keeping your shoulders steady. Your waist should expand like a balloon.
- Place the tip of your tongue behind your top front teeth.
- Whisper "tu" as you gradually blow a stream of air on your finger, as if cooling it. Make sure your lips are relaxed and rounded.
- Move your finger higher and lower. Try to keep the air stream blowing on it. Aim the air by moving your jaw, not by moving your head.

The air you feel is the air stream. It produces sound through the instrument. Your tongue is like a faucet or valve that releases or stops the air stream.

Your First Tone ▶

Your mouth's position on the instrument is called the embouchure (ahm' bah shure). Developing a good embouchure takes time and effort, so carefully follow these beginning steps:

- Hold the closed end of the head joint in your left hand. Cover the open end with the palm of your right hand.
- Rest the embouchure plate on your bottom lip. Center the embouchure hole on the center of your lips. The edge of the embouchure hole closest to you should rest on the dividing line between the red part of your lower lip and the skin of your chin. Look in a mirror!
- Keeping your upper and lower teeth slightly apart, draw the corners of your mouth straight back and relax your lower lip.

- Make a small opening in the center of your lips. Blow a stream of air into and across the embouchure hole. As you blow, slowly roll the head joint in and out until you find the embouchure position that produces your best clear and full tone. Slowly exhale your full air stream. Take another deep breath and try it again.

- You may become dizzy while playing. This is normal. You are taking more air into your lungs than normal and taking much longer to exhale. Just stop playing for a few minutes and breathe normally. After playing for a while, the dizziness will disappear.

Reading Music

Musical sounds are indicated by symbols called **notes** written on a **staff**. Notes come in several forms, but every note indicates **pitch** and **rhythm**.

The Staff

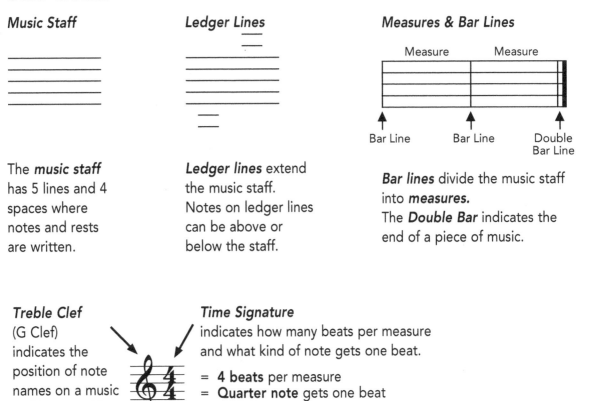

Music Staff

The **music staff** has 5 lines and 4 spaces where notes and rests are written.

Ledger Lines

Ledger lines extend the music staff. Notes on ledger lines can be above or below the staff.

Measures & Bar Lines

Measure   Measure

Bar Line   Bar Line   Double Bar Line

Bar lines divide the music staff into **measures.**
The **Double Bar** indicates the end of a piece of music.

Treble Clef
(G Clef) indicates the position of note names on a music staff: Second line is G.

Time Signature
indicates how many beats per measure and what kind of note gets one beat.

= **4 beats** per measure
= **Quarter note** gets one beat

Pitch

Pitch (the highness or lowness of a note) is indicated by the horizontal placement of the note on the staff. Notes higher on the staff are higher in pitch; notes lower on the staff are lower in pitch. To name the pitches, we use the first seven letters of the alphabet: A, B, C, D, E, F, and G. The **treble clef** (𝄞) assigns a particular pitch name to each line and space on the staff, centered around the pitch G, located on the second line of the staff. Music for the flute is always written in the treble clef. (Some instruments may make use of other clefs, which make the lines and spaces represent different pitches.)

Note Names

Each note is on a line or space of the staff. These note names are indicated by the Treble Clef.

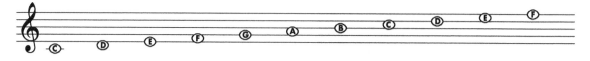

Sharps, Flats, and Naturals

These musical symbols are called accidentals which raise or lower the pitch of a note.

Sharp ♯ raises the note and remains in effect for the entire measure.

Flat ♭ lowers the note and remains in effect for the entire measure.

Natural ♮ cancels a flat (♭) or sharp (♯) and remains in effect for the entire measure.

Rhythm

Rhythm refers to how long, or for how many **beats** a note lasts. The beat is the pulse of music, and like your heartbeat it usually remains very steady. To help keep track of the beats in a piece of music, the staff is divided into **measures**. The **time signature** (numbers such as $\frac{4}{4}$ or $\frac{6}{8}$ at the beginning of the staff) indicates how many beats you will find in each measure. Counting the beats or tapping your foot can help to maintain a steady beat. Tap you foot down on each beat and up on each "&."

$\frac{4}{4}$ Time

Count:	1	&	2	&	3	&	4	&
Tap:	↓	↑	↓	↑	↓	↑	↓	↑

$\frac{4}{4}$ is probably the most common time signature. The **top number** tells you how many beats are in each measure; the **bottom number** tells you what kind of note receives one beat. In $\frac{4}{4}$ time there are four beats in the measure and a **quarter note** (♩ or ♪) equals one beat.

> 4 = **4 beats** per measure
> 4 = **Quarter note** gets one beat

Assembling Your Flute ▶

- To avoid damaging the keys during assembly/disassembly: Grasp the middle joint at the socket on top; and grasp the foot joint at the very bottom.

- Insert the head joint into the middle joint with a gentle twisting motion. Make sure the embouchure hole is directly in line with the middle joint's row of keys.

- Gently twist and insert the middle joint into the foot joint. The embouchure hole, the keys on the middle joint, and the long rod on the foot joint should all line up. (Refer to the picture under "The Parts of the Flute.")

How to Hold Your Flute

- Rest your left thumb on the long straight key on the underside of the flute. Curve your thumb in slightly. It is very important not to cramp your thumb by bending it backwards. Keep your wrist straight and let your fingers arch naturally over the center of the keys. The flute will rest lightly against the base of your first finger.

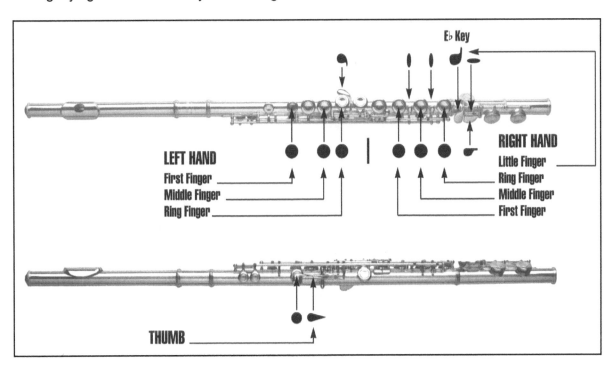

- Arch the fingers of your right hand and put them on the correct keys (your little finger will rest lightly on the E♭ key). Support the flute with your right thumb, which is placed on the underside of the flute between your first and second fingers.

- Holding the flute to your right, put it up to your mouth. You can think of your left hand as a pivot, with your right hand pushing gently forward and the embouchure plate pressing lightly against your lower lip. Hold the flute as shown.

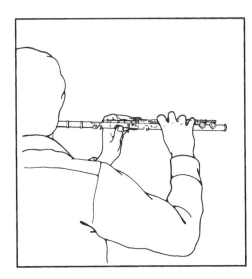

Putting Away Your Instrument

- Carefully shake any condensation out of your instrument.
- Using the cleaning rod, run a soft, clean cloth into the head joint and through the middle and foot joints.
- Carefully wipe the outside of each section to keep the finish clean. Never use silver polish to clean your flute.

Track 1

The First Note: F

To play "F", place your fingers on the keys as shown. The keys that are colored in should be pressed down.

Notes and Rests

Music uses symbols to indicated both the length of sound and of silence. Symbols indicating sound are called **Notes**. Symbols indicating silence are called **Rests**.

Whole Note/Whole Rest

A whole note means to play for four full beats (a complete measure in $\frac{4}{4}$ time). A whole rest means to be silent for four full beats.

Whole note	Half note	Quarter note	Eighth note
o	♩	♩	♪
Whole rest	Half rest	Quarter rest	Eighth rest
▬	▬	𝄽	𝄾

Listen to recorded track, then play along. Try to match the sound on the recording.

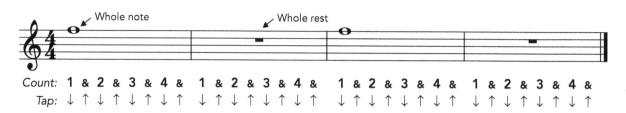

Track 2

Count and Play

Notes and Rests

Quarter Note/Quarter Rest

A quarter note means to play for one full beat. A quarter rest means to be silent for one full beat. There are four quarter notes or quarter rests in a $\frac{4}{4}$ measure.

Whole note	Half note	Quarter note	Eighth note
𝅝	𝅗𝅥	♩	♪
Whole rest	Half rest	Quarter rest	Eighth rest
𝄻	𝄼	𝄽	𝄾

Each note should begin with a quick "tu" to help separate it from the others.

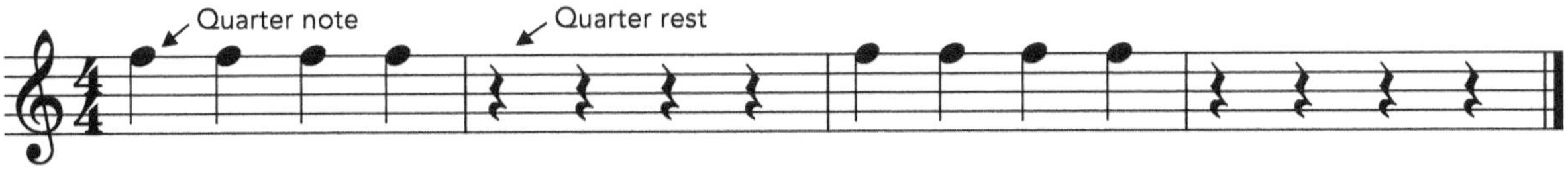

Count: 1 & 2 & 3 & 4 & 1 & 2 & 3 & 4 & 1 & 2 & 3 & 4 & 1 & 2 & 3 & 4 &

Tap: ↓ ↑ ↓ ↑ ↓ ↑ ↓ ↑ ↓ ↑ ↓ ↑ ↓ ↑ ↓ ↑ ↓ ↑ ↓ ↑ ↓ ↑ ↓ ↑ ↓ ↑ ↓ ↑ ↓ ↑ ↓ ↑

Don't just let the tracks play on. Repeat each exercise until you feel comfortable playing it by yourself and with the audio.

Track 3

A New Note: E♭ (E-flat)

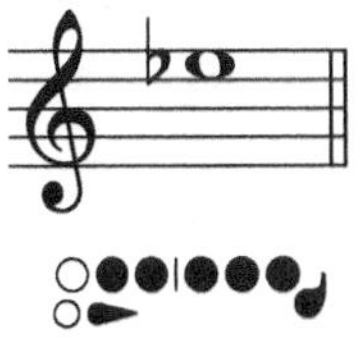

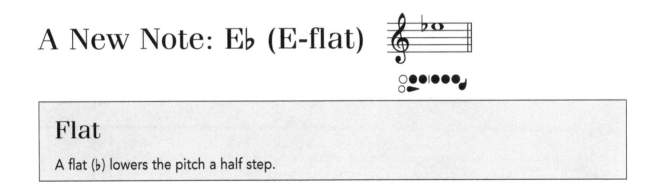

Flat

A flat (♭) lowers the pitch a half step.

Look for the fingering diagram under each new note. Practicing long tones like this will help to develop your sound and your breath control, so don't just move on to the next exercise. Repeat each one several times.

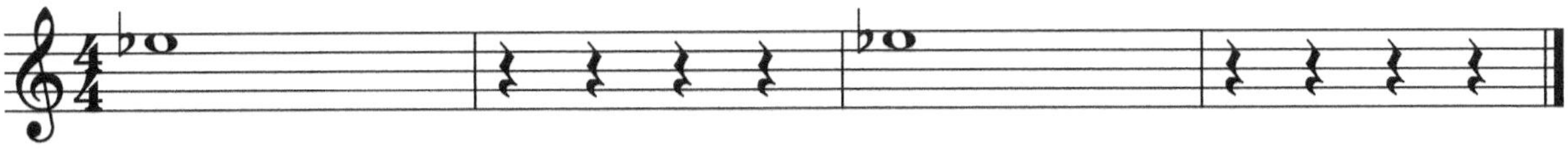

Count/ Tap: 1 & 2 & 3 & 4 & 1 & 2 & 3 & 4 & 1 & 2 & 3 & 4 & 1 & 2 & 3 & 4 &

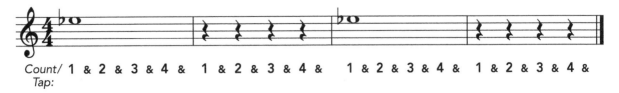

Track 4

Two's A Team

The flat sign (♭) remains in effect for the entire measure.

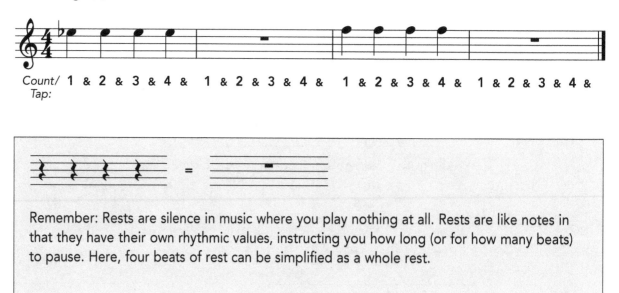

Count/ **1 & 2 & 3 & 4 & 1 & 2 & 3 & 4 & 1 & 2 & 3 & 4 & 1 & 2 & 3 & 4 &**
Tap:

Remember: Rests are silence in music where you play nothing at all. Rests are like notes in that they have their own rhythmic values, instructing you how long (or for how many beats) to pause. Here, four beats of rest can be simplified as a whole rest.

Track 5

A New Note: D

Count/ **1 & 2 & 3 & 4 & 1 & 2 & 3 & 4 & 1 & 2 & 3 & 4 & 1 & 2 & 3 & 4 &**
Tap:

Keeping Time

To keep a steady tempo, try tapping your foot and counting along with each song. In $\frac{4}{4}$ time, tap your foot four times in each measure and count, "1 & 2 & 3 & 4 &." Your foot should touch the floor on the number and come up on the "&." Each number and each "&" should be exactly the same duration, like the ticking of a clock.

Track 6

Moving On Up

If you become winded or dizzy your air stream is probably too warm and the opening between your lips is too large. You can still practice by fingering the notes on your instrument and singing the pitches or counting the rhythm out loud.

Count/ **1 & 2 & 3 & 4 & 1 & 2 & 3 & 4 & 1 & 2 & 3 & 4 & 1 & 2 & 3 & 4 &**
Tap:

Track 7

A New Note: C

Count/
Tap: 1 & 2 & 3 & 4 & 1 & 2 & 3 & 4 & 1 & 2 & 3 & 4 & 1 & 2 & 3 & 4 &

Track 8

Four By Four

Repeat Signs

Repeat signs 𝄆 𝄇 tell you to repeat everything between them. If only the sign on the right appears (𝄇), repeat from the beginning of the piece.

Repeat sign ↘

Count/
Tap: 1 & 2 & 3 & 4 & 1 & 2 & 3 & 4 & 1 & 2 & 3 & 4 & 1 & 2 & 3 & 4 &

Track 9

A New Note: B♭

Count/
Tap: 1 & 2 & 3 & 4 & 1 & 2 & 3 & 4 &   1 & 2 & 3 & 4 & 1 & 2 & 3 & 4 &

Track 10

The Fab Five

1 & 2 & 3 & 4 & 1 & 2 & 3 & 4 & 1 & 2 & 3 & 4 & 1 & 2 & 3 & 4 &

Track 11

First Flight

Keep the beat steady by silently counting or tapping while you play.

Track 12

Rolling Along

Tonguing

To start each note, whisper the syllable "tu." Keep the air stream going continuously and touch the tip of your tongue against your upper teeth for each new note. If the notes change, be sure to move your fingers quickly so that each note will come out cleanly. When you come to a rest or the end of the song, just stop blowing. Using your tongue to stop the air will cause an abrupt and unpleasant ending of the sound.

- Play long tones to warm up at the beginning of every practice session.
- Tap, count out loud and sing through each exercise with the track before you play it.
- Play each exercise several times until you feel comfortable with it.

Track 13

Hot Cross Buns

Notes and Rests

Half Note/Half Rest

A half note means to play for two full beats. (It's equal in length to two quarter notes.) A half rest means to be silent for two beats. There are two half notes or half rests in a $\frac{4}{4}$ measure.

Whole note	Half note	Quarter note	Eighth note
o	♩	♩	♪
Whole rest	Half rest	Quarter rest	Eighth rest
▬	▬	𝄽	𝄾

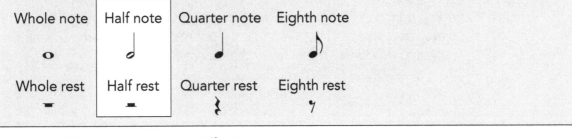

Track 14

Go Tell Aunt Rhodie

Breath Mark

The breath mark (ʼ) indicates a specific place to inhale. Play the proceeding note for the full length then take a deep, quick breath through your mouth.

Remember to keep the center of your lips relaxed! Make certain that your cheeks don't puff out when you blow. Bring your jaw back as you descend and forward as you ascend.

The Whole Thing

Track 15

Remember: a whole rest (-) indicates a whole measure of silence. Note that the whole rest hangs down from the 4th line, whereas the half rest sits on the 3rd line.

March Steps

Track 16

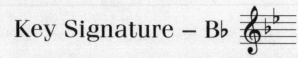

Key Signature – B♭

A **key signature** (the group of sharps or flats before the time signature) tells which notes are played as sharps or flats throughout the entire piece. In this exercise, all the B's and E's are played as B♭ and E♭. [This is called the **Key of B♭**.]

Key signature

Lightly Row

Track 17

Always be sure to check the key signature before starting a new song.

Track 18

Reaching Higher (New Note: G)

Fermata

The fermata (⌢) indicates that a note or rest is held somewhat longer than normal.

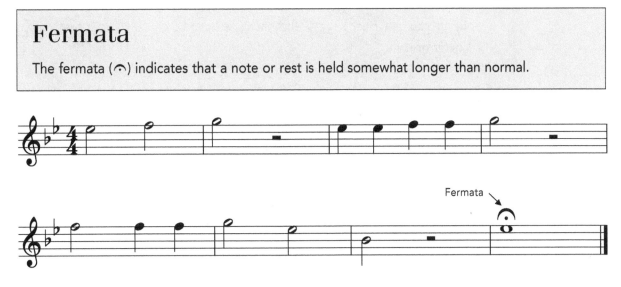

Track 19

Au Claire De La Lune

Track 20

Twinkle, Twinkle Little Star

- Keep your lips soft and relaxed.   • Keep your throat open and free from tension.
- Work for a narrow, rapid stream of air.   • Keep your chin parallel to the floor for good focus.
- Bring your jaw back slightly and have your top lip closer to your teeth as you progress to the lower notes.

Track 21

Deep Pockets (New Note: A)

Always practice long tones on each new note.

Track 22

Doodle All Day

Breath Support

In order to play in tune and with a full, beautiful tone, it is necessary to breathe properly and control the air as you play. Quickly take the breath in through your mouth all the way to the bottom of your lungs. Then tighten your stomach muscles and push the air quickly through the flute, controlling the air with your lips. Practice this by forming your lips as you do when you play and then blowing against your hand. If the air is cool, you are doing it correctly. If the air is warm, tighten the lips and make the air stream smaller. Keep the air stream moving fast at all times, especially as you begin to run out of air. Practice blowing against your hand and see how long you can keep the air going. Work to keep the air stream from beginning to end.

Now try this with your flute. Select a note that is comfortable to play and see how long you can hold it. Listen carefully to yourself to see if the tone gets louder or softer, changes pitch slightly, or if the quality of the tone changes. Do this a few times every time you practice, trying to hold the note a little longer each time and maintain a good sound.

Track 23

Jingle Bells

Dynamics

Dynamics refer to how loud or soft the music is. Traditionally, many musical terms (including dynamic markings) are called by their Italian names:

f	forte *(four' tay)*	loud
mf	mezzo forte *(met' zoh four' tay)*	moderately loud
p	piano *(pee ahn' oh)*	soft

Producing a louder sound requires more air, but you should use full breath support at all dynamic levels.

Track 24

My Dreydl

Pick-up Notes

Sometimes there are notes that come before the first full measure. They are called *pick-up notes*. Often, when a song begins with a pick-up measure, the note's value (in beats) is subtracted from the last measure. To play this song with a one beat pick-up, you count "1, 2, 3" and start playing on beat 4.

One-beat pick-up note

Last measure has 3 beats, not 4

Track 25

Eighth Note Jam

Notes and Rests

Eighth Note/Eighth Rest

An eighth note is half the value of a quarter note, that is, half a beat. An eighth rest means to be silent for half a beat. There are eight eighth notes or eight eighth rests in a $\frac{4}{4}$ measure.

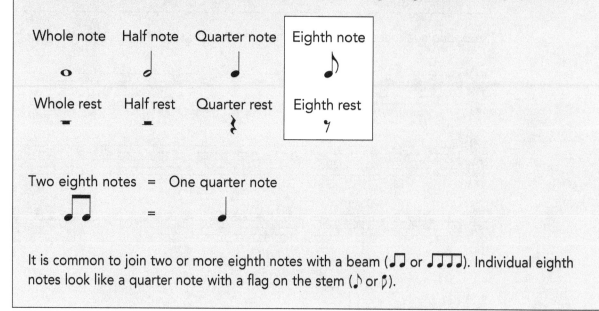

Whole note	Half note	Quarter note	Eighth note
o	𝅗𝅥	♩	♪

Whole rest	Half rest	Quarter rest	Eighth rest
▬	▬	𝄽	𝄾

Two eighth notes = One quarter note

It is common to join two or more eighth notes with a beam (♫ or ♬). Individual eighth notes look like a quarter note with a flag on the stem (♪ or ♩).

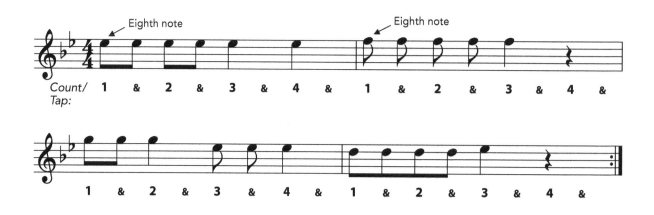

Count/Tap: 1 & 2 & 3 & 4 & 1 & 2 & 3 & 4 &

1 & 2 & 3 & 4 & 1 & 2 & 3 & 4 &

Eighth Note Counting

The first eighth note comes on "1" as your foot taps the floor. The second happens as your foot moves up on "&." The third is on "2" and the fourth is on the next "&" and so forth. Remember to count and tap in a steady and even manner, like the ticking of a clock.

Skip To My Lou

Remember to keep the left first finger raised on "D" and "E♭."

Long, Long Ago

Good posture will improve your sound. Avoid lifting your head too high.

Oh, Susanna

Notice the pick-up notes.

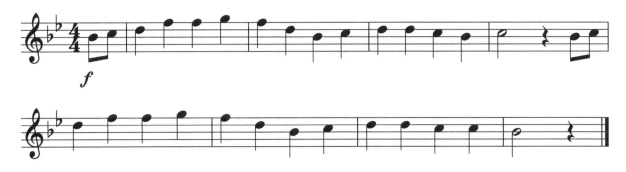

William Tell

- Balance the flute at the base of the first finger of your left hand.
- Curve your fingers so the fleshy part of the finger tip touches the center of the key.

Track 30

Two By Two

$\frac{2}{4}$ Time

A time signature of $\frac{2}{4}$ means that a quarter note gets one beat, but there are only two beats in a measure.

Count/   **1 & 2 &**   **1 & 2 &**   **1 & 2 &**   **1 & 2 &**   **1 & 2 &**   **1 & 2 &**   **1 & 2 &**   **1 & 2 &**
Tap:

Track 31

High School Cadets March

Tempo Markings

The speed or pace of music is called **tempo**. Tempo markings are usually written above the staff. Many of these terms come from the Italian.

Allegro	*(ah lay' grow)*	Fast tempo
Moderato	*(mah der ah' tow)*	Medium or moderate tempo
Andante	*(ahn dahn' tay)*	Slower "walking" tempo

Track 32

Hey, Ho! Nobody's Home (New Note: G)

Octaves

Notes that have the same name but are eight notes higher or lower are called **octaves**. You already knew how to play a G, but this new G is one octave lower. Practice playing both G's one after the other like this:

The higher notes will be played more easily if you:

- With your lips, make the air stream round rather than flat.
- Move your jaw slightly forward so the high stream is directed a little higher.
- Blow the air slightly faster.

Track 33

Play The Dynamics

Dynamics

Gradual changes in volume are indicated by these symbols:

    Crescendo (gradually louder)   sometimes abbreviated *cresc.*

    Decrescendo or *Diminuendo* (gradually softer)   sometimes abbreviated *dim.*

Remember to keep the air stream moving fast both as you get louder by gradually using more air on the crescendo, *and* as you get softer by gradually using less air on the decrescendo.

Track 34

Aura Lee

21

Frère Jacques

Hard Rock Blues

Posture

Good body posture will allow you to take in a full, deep breath and control the air better as you play. Sit or stand with your spine straight and tall. Your shoulders should be back and relaxed. Keep your jaw parallel to the floor and don't let your right arm drop down. Think about your posture as you begin playing and check it several times while playing.

Track 37

Alouette

Tie

A *tie* is a curved line connecting two notes of the same pitch. It indicates that instead of playing both notes, you play the first note and hold it for the total time value of both notes.

 = 2 beats

Dot

A *dot* adds half the value of the note to which it is attached. A dotted half note (♩.) has a total time value of three beats:

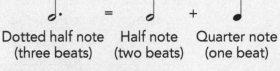

Dotted half note (three beats)   Half note (two beats)   Quarter note (one beat)

Therefore, a dotted half note has exactly the same value as a half note tied to a quarter note. Playing track 37 again, compare this music to the previous example:

New Directions (New Note: F)

Track 38

This F is an octave lower than the F you already know. Once again, practice going from one F to the other. To play the low notes more easily:

- Direct the air stream lower into the embouchure hole by bringing your jaw back and keeping your top lip closer to your top teeth.
- Blow more softly than you did for higher notes.
- Make the opening in your lips more flat than round.

The Nobles

Track 39

Ties are useful when you need to extend the value of a note across a bar line. Notice the tie across the bar line between the first and second measure. The F on the third beat is held through the following beats 4 and 1.

Track 40

Three Beat Jam

$\frac{3}{4}$ Time

The next song is in $\frac{3}{4}$ time signature. That is, three beats (quarter notes) per measure.

$\frac{3}{4}$ time feels very different from $\frac{4}{4}$ time. Putting more emphasis on the first beat of each measure will help you feel the new meter.

Track 41

Morning (from Peer Gynt)

Hand and Finger Position

Now is a good time to go back to page 7 and review proper hand and finger position. This is very important to proper technique. Keeping the fingers curved and close to their assigned keys will allow your fingers and hands to be relaxed and will aid in getting from one note to another quickly, easily, and accurately. The further you lift your fingers off the keys, the more likely that you will put them down on the wrong key or not securely close the key. Besides that, fingers pointing in all directions doesn't look good!

- As you finger the notes on your flute, you can practice quietly by speaking the names of the notes, counting out the rhythms, or singing or whistling the pitches.
- Don't let your cheeks puff out when you play.

Track 42

Mexican Clapping Song ("Chiapanecas")

Accent

The accent (>) means you should emphasize the note to which it is attached. Do this by using a more explosive "t" on the "tu" with which you produce the note.

Track 43

Hot Muffins (New Note: A♭)

Sharps, Flats, and Naturals

Any sharp (♯), flat (♭), or natural (♮) sign that appears in the music but is not in the key signature is called an *accidental*. The accidental in the next example is an A♭ and it effects all of the A's for the rest of the measure.

A **sharp** (♯) raises the pitch of a note by one half step.
A **flat** (♭) lowers the pitch of a note by one half step.
A **natural** (♮) cancels a previous sharp or flat, returning a note to its original pitch.

When a song requires a note to be a half step higher or lower, you'll see a sharp (♯), flat (♭), or natural (♮) sign in front of it. This tells you to raise or lower the note *for that measure only*. We'll see more of these "accidentals" as we continue learning more notes on the flute.

Cossack Dance

Notice the repeat sign at the end of the fourth measure. Although this particular repeat sign does not occur at the end of the exercise, it behaves just like any other repeat sign. Play the repeated section twice, then continue.

Track 45

Basic Blues (New Note: A♭)

Track 46

High Flying

Key Signature – E♭

The **Key of E♭** means to play all B's as B-flats, all E's as E-flats, and all A's as A-flats.

1st and 2nd Endings

The use of **1st and 2nd endings** is a variant on the basic repeat sign. You play through the music to the repeat sign and repeat as always, but the second time through the music, skip the measure or measures under the "first ending" and go directly to the "second ending."

Up On A Housetop

Allegro

The Big Airstream (New Note: B♭)

Track 48

Waltz Theme

Track 49

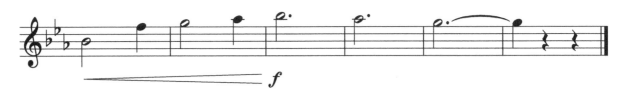

Down By The Station

Track 50

Banana Boat Song

D.C. al Fine

At the **D.C. al Fine**, play again from the beginning, stopping at **Fine**. D.C. is the abbreviation for Da Capo *(dah cah' poh),* which means "to the beginning." Fine *(fee' neh)* means "the end."

Track 52

Razor's Edge (New Note: E)

Natural Sign

A natural sign (♮) cancels a flat or a sharp for the remainder of the measure.

Natural sign

Track 53

The Music Box

Key Signature – C

The absence of a key signature indicates that all notes are played as naturals, neither sharps or flats. This is the **Key of C**.

Moderato

Slur

A curved line connecting notes of different pitch is called a **slur**. Notice the difference between a slur and a tie, which connects notes of the **same** pitch.

Only tongue the first note of a slur. As you finger the next note, keep the breath going. You must precisely change the fingering from one note to the next to prevent extraneous pitches from sounding.

Track 54

Smooth Operator

Track 55

Gliding Along

This exercise is almost identical to the previous one. Notice how the different slurs change the tonguing.

Track 56

Take The Lead (New Note: A)

Remember to practice the octaves when you learn a new note.

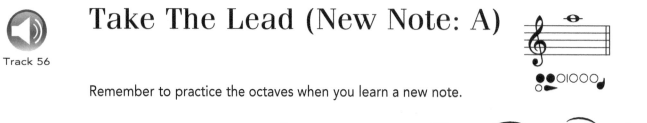

The Cold Wind

Track 57

Phrase

A phrase is a musical "sentence," often 2 or 4 measures long. Try to play a phrase in one breath.

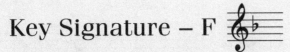

Satin Latin

Track 58

Key Signature – F

A key signature with one flat indicates that all written B's should be played as B♭'s.
This is the **Key of F**.

Multiple Measure Rest

Sometimes you won't play for several measures. The number above the **multiple measure rest** (▬) indicates how many full measures to rest. Count through the silent measures.

Track 59

March Militaire (New Note: E)

Track 60

The Flat Zone (New Note: D♭)

Track 61

On Top Of Old Smokey

All Through The Night

Dotted Quarter Note

Remember that a dot adds half the value of the note. A dotted quarter note followed by a eighth note (♩. ♪) and (♩ ♪♪) have the same rhythmic value.

Sea Chanty

Scarborough Fair

Track 64

Auld Lang Syne

Track 65

- For the lower notes, bring the jaw and lips back, blow more softly and direct the air stream lower into the embouchure hole.

- For the higher notes, move the jaw and lips forward, use more air and aim your air stream slightly higher.

- Since lower tones tend to be softer than higher tones, be sure to give enough strength to the lower tones. Don't smother the sound by lowering your head or rolling the flute in too far.

- Play smoothly and evenly by keeping your fingers close to the keys at all times.

- If you keep your jaw parallel to the floor, your high "C" will respond nicely.

Track 66

Crossing Over (New Note: C)

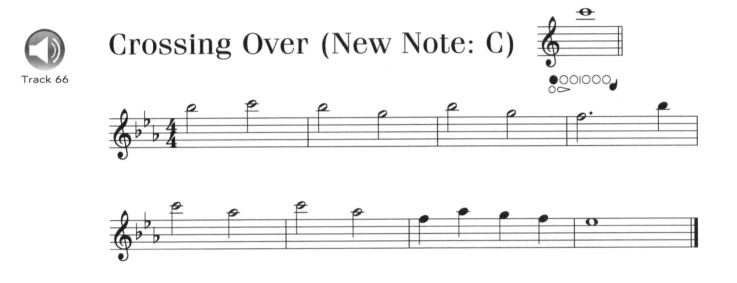

Track 67

Michael Row The Boat Ashore

Repeat the section of music enclosed by the repeat signs (‖ ‖). If 1st and 2nd endings are used, they are played as usual—but go back only to the first repeat sign, not to the beginning.

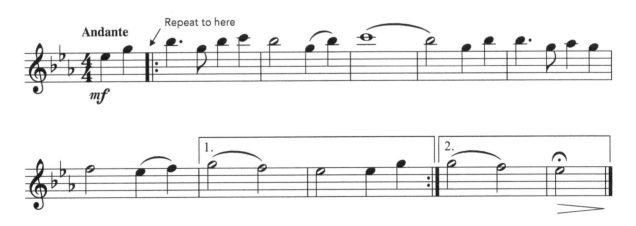

Track 68

Botany Bay

Track 69

Finlandia

𝄴 Time Signature

Common time (𝄴) is the same as $\frac{4}{4}$.

When The Saints Go Marching In

The Streets of Laredo

A Quick Review

Posture

Whether sitting on the edge of your chair or standing, you should always keep your:

- Spine straight and tall,
- Shoulders back and relaxed, and
- Feet flat on the floor.

Holding Your Flute

- The flute rests on the little "shelf" formed at the base of the left index finger. Be certain that your thumb is curved in, not bent back.

- Keep your fingers arched comfortably, lightly touching the center of the keys. Your hands should always be relaxed. Tensing up your hand will limit your dexterity.

- Hold the flute straight out to the right, and place the embouchure plate under your bottom lip. The edge of the embouchure hole closest to you should rest under the dividing line between the red part of your lower lip and the skin of your chin. Think of your left hand as a pivot point and with your right hand, push out gently so that the embouchure plate presses in lightly against your chin.

Taking Care of Your Instrument

- **Never** use silver polish to clean your flute. Just wipe it with a soft cloth after each practice session. Avoid polishing between the keys.

- Be sure to set the flute down with the keys facing upward. Otherwise the moisture inside the flute can run onto the pads and make them stick.

- Wipe the inside of your flute dry at the end of each practice session. Insert a soft cloth in the slot of the cleaning rod and pull it through each joint of your flute. Doubling the cloth over the top of the rod will prevent scratching the inside of your instrument and will help to remove all moisture from inside the head joint around the cork.

- The cork inside the closed end of the head joint is very delicate. Do not turn the cap that is on this end because it will move the cork and throw the instrument out of tune. Be careful not to push the cleaning rod hard against the cork when you clean the flute.

Lesson 11

Warm-ups

Like athletes, musicians need to "warm up" before they perform. A good warm-up will loosen up the muscles of the embouchure and tongue, relax the hands, and focus your mind on playing the instrument. The next three tracks are good warm-up exercises that should be played every day. Before each exercise, take a full and comfortable breath. Work for a smooth, steady tone.

Track 72

Range and Flexibility Builder

Track 73

Technique Trax

Track 74

More Technique Trax

- Play smoothly and evenly by keeping your fingers close to the keys at all times.

- If you cover too much of the embouchure hole, you will not have enough room to adjust the pitch of your tone. To correct this cover less of the embouchure hole with your lower lip.

- Since lower tones naturally tend to be softer than higher tones, be sure to give enough strength to lower notes. Do not smother them by lowering your head or rolling the flute in too far. Bring your jaw inward and point your top lip downward to improve low note focus and response.

Track 75

Eighth Note March

Eighth Note/Rest

Recall that an eighth note (♪ or ♪) gets ½ of one beat. An equivalent period of silence is represented by an *eighth rest* (𝄾).

Track 76

Minuet

Track 77

Eighth Notes Off the Beat

1 & 2 & 3 & 4 &   1 & 2 & 3 & 4 &   1 & 2 & 3 & 4 &   1 & 2 & 3 & 4 &

Track 78

Eighth Note Scramble

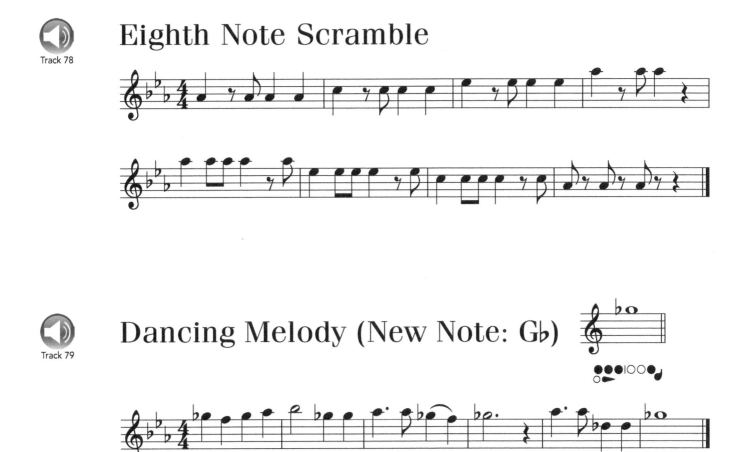

Track 79

Dancing Melody (New Note: G♭)

Track 80

El Capitan

Ready for a quick lesson in music theory? A *scale* is a sequence of notes in ascending or descending order. Like a musical "ladder," each step is the next consecutive note in the key. The scale in the key of C is a specific pattern of **half steps** and **whole steps** (more on this later) between one C and another C an **octave** higher or lower.

The same pattern of half steps and whole steps beginning on a different pitch would produce a different key with a different key signature.

The distance between two pitches is called an *interval*. Starting with "1" on the lower note, count each line and space between the notes. The number of the higher note is the distance of the interval. A whole step or half step is called a **second**, the interval between steps 1 and 3 is called a **third**, and so on. Notice that the interval between scale steps 4 and 6, for example, is also a third.

You already know a sharp raises the pitch of a note. Now you know a sharp raises the pitch of a note by a half-step. Similarly, a flat lowers the pitch of a note one half-step. Two notes that are written differently, but sound the same (and are played with the same fingering) are called enharmonics.

Track 81

Dark Shadows – G♭/F♯

Notice the F♯ in the second full measure (that is, not counting the partial measure with the pick-up note). It is the same pitch and is played with the same fingering as the G♭ in the fourth measure.

Pick-up note

Track 82

Notes in Disguise – D♭/C♯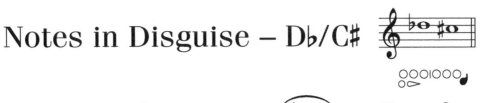

Track 83

Half-Steppin'

Chromatic Scale

At the beginning of this lesson, we saw examples of half steps and whole steps. The smallest distance between two notes is a half-step. A scale made up of consecutive half-steps is called a **chromatic scale**.

Track 84

March Slav

Largo

Largo *(lahr' goh)* is a tempo indication that means "slow and solemn."

Track 85

Egyptian Dance

Track 86

Chroma-Zone

Track 87

Technique Trax

- To play more loudly, blow the air stream more rapidly across the embouchure hole. To keep the pitch uniform, aim the air stream slightly lower and relax your lips to allow for free passage of the extra air.

- To play more softly, decrease the speed of the air stream and direct it slightly higher across the embouchure hole.

Track 88

Treading Lightly

Staccato

Staccato (*sta kah' toe*) notes are played lightly and with separation. They are marked with a dot above or below the note. Shorten each note by stopping the air stream.

Track 89

Smooth Move

Tenuto

Tenuto (*tih noo' toe*) notes are played smoothly and connected, holding each note for its full value until the next is played. They are marked with a straight line above or below the note.

Shifting Gears

Technique Trax

Grandfather's Clock

Glow Worm

Allegretto, Ritardando

There are two new terms in this exercise. *Allegretto* (ahl ih gret' toh) is a tempo indication, usually a little slower than Allegro and with a lighter style. *Ritardando* (rih tar dahn' doh) means the tempo gradually gets slower. It is usually abbreviated *rit.* or *ritard*.

Paul Lincke

Alma Mater

Track 94

Loch Lomond

Track 95

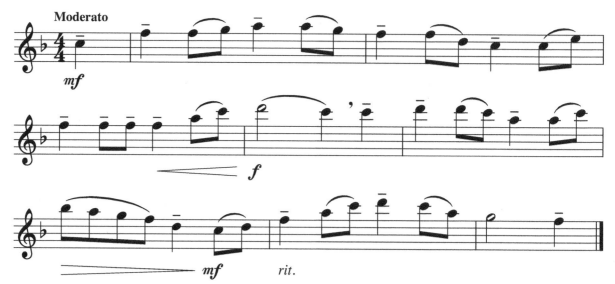

Molly Malone

Track 96

Key Change

The key can change in the middle of a piece. You will usually see a double bar line and a new key signature at the **key change**. You may also see natural signs reminding you to "cancel" previous sharps and flats.

Key Change

A Cut Above

Alla Breve

Alla Breve (ah' la bra' ve), commonly called **cut time**, has a time signature of ¢ or ²⁄₂. The top "2" indicates two beats per measure. The bottom "2" means a half note (♩), not a quarter note, gets one beat. Of course, this means a whole note (o) receives two beats and a quarter note (♩) only gets ½ beat.

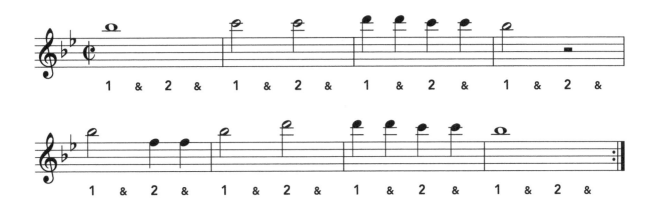

Track 98

Yankee Doodle

First, play the version in ²⁄₄. Then repeat the track and play the cut time version. Is there any difference?

The Victors

Notice the ♩. ♪ patterns. In cut time, the dotted half note receives 1½ beats and the quarter note receives ½ beat.

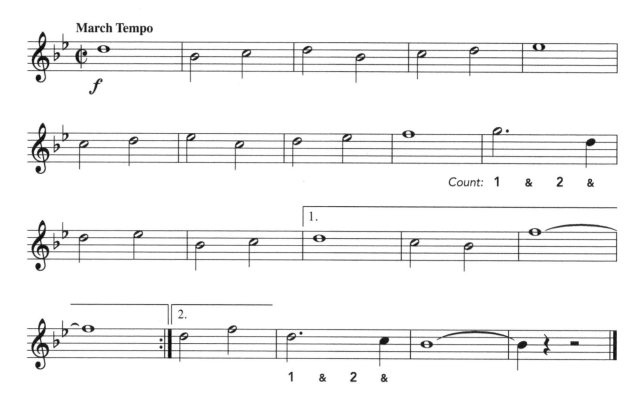

Track 100

A-Roving

Mezzo Piano

We have already seen dynamic markings such as *p*, *mf*, and *f*. **Mezzo piano** (*met' zo pee ahn' no*), abbreviated *mp*, means moderately soft: a little louder than piano, not as loud as mezzo forte.

Remember to use a full breath support at all dynamic levels.

Track 101

In Sync

Syncopation

Generally, the notes **on** the beat (that's the 1's, 2's, 3's and such) are played a bit stronger or louder than the notes on the **off-beats** (that's the &'s). When an accent or emphasis is given to a note that is not normally on a strong beat, it is called **syncopation**. This sort of "off-beat" feel is common in many popular and classical styles.

La Roca

You're A Grand Old Flag

Rehearsal Numbers

In longer pieces, the publisher sometimes includes *rehearsal numbers* to help the conductor or band leader start and stop the ensemble easily. Sometimes they are letters like A, B, C; sometimes numbers like 1, 2, 3. Frequently, such as here, they are measure numbers.

Crescendo, Decrescendo

A gradual increase in volume is called *crescendo* (kreh shen' doh). It is usually indicated by *cresc.* or ◁. A corresponding gradual decrease in volume is called *decrescendo* (deh kre shen' do), abbreviated *decresc.*, or *diminuendo* (dih meh nyu ehn' doh), abbreviated *dim*. A decrescendo (diminuendo) may be represented by ▷.

George M. Cohan

The Minstrel Boy (New Note: B)

Track 104

Notice the key signature: the key of C. No sharps or flats.

Close Call (New Note: B)

Track 105

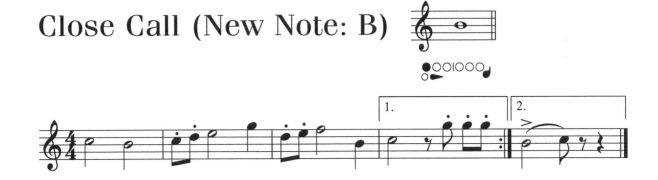

Winning Streak

Track 106

Pay attention to the syncopation. It is similar to what you played earlier, but now the time signature is ¢.

Sixteenth Note Fanfare

Sixteenth Notes

A sixteenth note (𝅘𝅥𝅯 or ♪) has half the value of an eighth note. In $\frac{4}{4}$, $\frac{3}{4}$, or $\frac{2}{4}$ time, four sixteenth notes (𝅘𝅥𝅯𝅘𝅥𝅯𝅘𝅥𝅯𝅘𝅥𝅯) get one beat.

Moving Along

Comin' Round The Mountain Variations

Track 110

Sea Chantey

Observe that an eighth note and two sixteenths are normally written ♪♬. This has the same rhythmic pattern as ♪♬♩.

Track 111

American Fanfare (New Note: D♭)

Maestoso

Maestoso (mah ee stoh' soh) means "majestic, stately, and dignified."

Track 112

Scale Study

This new key signature indicates the key of A♭. The first four measures consist of the A♭ scale.

Bill Bailey

Moderato

Rhythm Etude

Track 114

Observe that two sixteenth notes followed by an eighth are normally written ♫♪. This has the same rhythmic pattern as ♪♫♪.

Celtic Dance

Track 115

The Galway Piper

Track 116

Marching Along

The figures ♪♫ and ♩.♫ are equivalent.

S'vivon

Track 119

Toreador Song

Track 120

La Cumparsita (New Note: G♭/F♯)

Track 121

The Yellow Rose Of Texas

Check the key signature.

Track 122

Scale Study (New Note: E♭)

Track 123

American Patrol

Aria (from Marriage of Figaro)

The Stars And Stripes Forever

John Philip Sousa

Track 126

Lazy Day

$\frac{6}{8}$ Time

Now you will be introduced to a new time signature: $\frac{6}{8}$. The "6" on top indicates that there are six beats per measure. The "8" on the bottom indicates that the eighth note gets one beat. If the eighth note (♪) gets one beat, then it follows that a dotted quarter note (♩.) receives three beats and a dotted half note (♩.) gets six.

$\frac{6}{8}$ time is usually played with slight emphasis on the 1st and 4th beats of each measure. This divides the measure into two groups of three beats each.

1 2 3 **4** 5 6   **1** 2 3 **4** 5 6   **1** 2 3 **4** 5 6   **1** 2 3 **4** 5 6

Track 127

Row Your Boat

Jolly Good Fellow

Track 128

When Johnny Comes Marching Home

In faster music, the primary beats in $\frac{6}{8}$ time (beats 1 and 4) will make the music feel like it's counted in "2," but with a *triple subdivision* of the beat rather than *duple*.

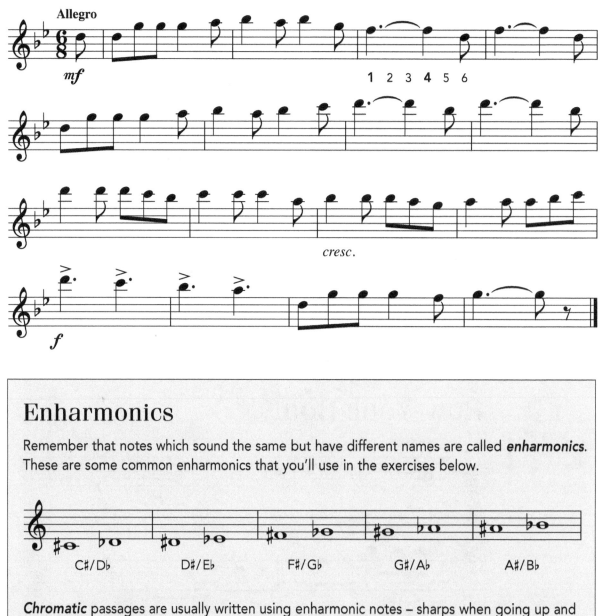

Enharmonics

Remember that notes which sound the same but have different names are called **enharmonics**. These are some common enharmonics that you'll use in the exercises below.

C♯/D♭ D♯/E♭ F♯/G♭ G♯/A♭ A♯/B♭

Chromatic passages are usually written using enharmonic notes – sharps when going up and flats when going down.

Chromatic Scale

Practice slowly until you are sure of all the fingerings.

Technique Trax

Chromatic Crescendo

Staccato Study

Yankee Doodle Dandy

Track 134

George M. Cohan

Allegro

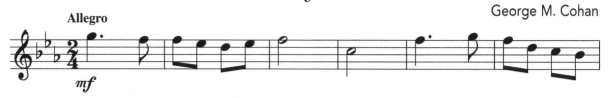

Three To Get Ready

Track 135

> ## Triplet
>
> A *triplet* is a group of 3 notes played in the time usually occupied by 2. In $\frac{2}{4}$, $\frac{3}{4}$, or $\frac{4}{4}$ time, an eighth note triplet (♪♪♪) is spread evenly across one beat.

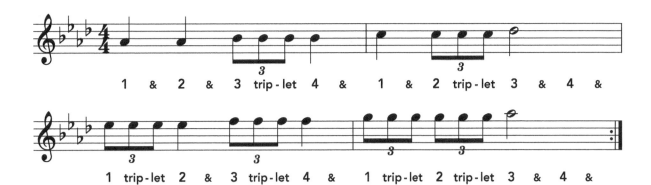

1   &   2   &   3 trip-let 4   &   1   &   2 trip-let 3   &   4   &

1 trip-let 2   &   3 trip-let 4   &   1 trip-let 2 trip-let 3   &   4   &

Triplet Study

Track 136

Theme From Faust

Track 137

Maestoso

69

Over The River And Through The Woods

New Notes: E   F

Track 139

On The Move

Higher Ground

Track 140

Doodle All Day

Track 141

D.S. March

Track 142

D.S. al Fine

Play until you see **D.S. al Fine**. Then go back to the sign (𝄋) and play until the word **Fine**.
D.S. is the abbreviation for **Dal Segno** (dahl say' nio), which is Italian for "from the sign," and
Fine (fee' nay) means "the end."

Track 143

Tarantella

Track 144

Emperor Waltz

Andantino

Andantino (ahn dahn tee' noh) is a tempo between Andante and Moderato.

Track 145

Unfinished Symphony Theme

> ## Legato
>
> **Legato** *(leh gah' toh)* means to play in a smooth, graceful manner, almost as if everything was slurred.

Track 146

Greensleeves

Flute Scales and Arpeggios

Key of B♭

1.

2.

3.

4.

Flute Scales and Arpeggios

Key of E♭

1.

2.

3.

4.

Flute Scales and Arpeggios

Key of F

1.

2.

3.

4.

Choose the upper or lower notes to play.

Flute Scales and Arpeggios

Key of C

1.

2.

3.

4.

Flute Scales and Arpeggios

Key of A♭

1.

2.

3.

4.

Fingering Chart for Flute

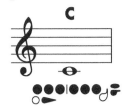

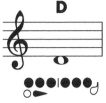

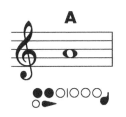

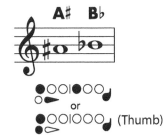

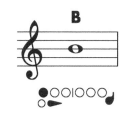

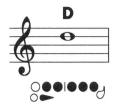

Fingering Chart for Flute

Glossary of Musical Terms

Accent	An Accent mark (>) means you should emphasize the note to which it is attached.
Accidental	Any sharp (♯), flat (♭), or natural (♮) sign that appears in the music but is not in the key signature is called an Accidental.
Alla Breve	Commonly called cut time, has a time signature of ₵ or $\frac{2}{2}$.
Allegretto	A tempo indication usually a little slower than Allegro and with a lighter style.
Allegro	Fast tempo.
Andante	Slower "walking" tempo.
Andantino	A tempo between Andante and Moderato.
Arpeggio	An Arpeggio is a "broken" chord whose notes are played individually.
Bass Clef (𝄢)	(F Clef) indicates the position of note names on a music staff: The fourth line in Bass Clef is F.
Bar Lines	Bar Lines divide the music staff into measures.
Beat	The Beat is the pulse of music, and like a heartbeat it should remain very steady. Counting aloud and foot-tapping help maintain a steady beat.
Breath Mark	The Breath Mark (,) indicates a specific place to inhale. Play the proceeding note for the full length then take a deep, quick breath through your mouth.
Chord	When two or more notes are played together, they form a Chord or harmony.
Chromatic Notes	Chromatic Notes are altered with sharps, flats and natural signs which are not in the key signature.
Chromatic Scale	The smallest distance between two notes is a half-step, and a scale made up of consecutive half-steps is called a Chromatic Scale.
Common Time	Common Time (𝄴) is the same as $\frac{4}{4}$ time signature.
Crescendo	Play gradually louder. (*cresc.*)
D.C. al Fine	D.C. al Fine means to play again from the beginning, stopping at Fine. D.C. is the abbreviation for Da Capo, or "to the beginning," and Fine means "the end."
D.S. al Fine	Play until you see D.S. al Fine. Then go back to the sign (𝄋) and play until the word Fine. D.S. is the abbreviation for Dal Segno, which is Italian for "from the sign," and Fine means "the end."
Decrescendo	Play gradually softer. (*decresc.*)

Glossary continued

Diminuendo	Same as decrescendo. (*dim.*)
Dotted Half Note	A note three beats long in duration (𝅗𝅥.). A dot adds half the value of the note.
Dotted Quarter Note	A note one and a half beats long in duration (♩.). A dot adds half the value of the note.
Double Bar (‖)	Indicates the end of a piece of music.
Duet	A composition with two different parts played together.
Dynamics	Dynamics indicate how loud or soft to play a passage of music. Remember to use full breath support to control your tone at all dynamic levels.
Eighth Note	An Eighth Note (♪) receives half the value of a quarter note, that is, half a beat. Two or more eighth notes are usually joined together with a beam, like this: ♫
Eighth Rest	Indicates 1/2 beat of silence. (𝄾)
Embouchure	Your mouth's position on the mouthpiece of the instrument.
Enharmonics	Two notes that are written differently, but sound the same (and played with the same fingering) are called Enharmonics.
Fermata	The Fermata (𝄐) indicates that a note (or rest) is held somewhat longer than normal.
1st & 2nd Endings	The use of 1st and 2nd Endings is a variant on the basic repeat sign. You play through the music to the repeat sign and repeat as always, but the second time through the music, skip the measure or measures under the "first ending" and go directly to the "second ending."
Flat (♭)	Lowers the note a half step and remains in effect for the entire measure.
Forte (*f*)	Play loudly.
Half Note	A Half Note (𝅗𝅥) receives two beats. It's equal in length to two quarter notes.
Half Rest	The Half Rest (▬) marks two beats of silence.
Harmony	Two or more notes played together. Each combination forms a chord.
Interval	The distance between two pitches is an Interval.
Key Change	When a song changes key you will usually see a double bar line and the new key signature at the key change. You may also see natural signs reminding you to "cancel" previous sharps and flats.
Key Signature	A Key Signature (the group of sharps or flats before the time signature) tells which notes are played as sharps or flats throughout the entire piece.
Largo	Play very slow.

Ledger Lines	Ledger Lines extend the music staff. Notes on ledger lines can be above or below the staff.
Legato	Legato means to play in a smooth, graceful manner, almost as if everything was slurred.
Mezzo Forte (*mf*)	Play moderately loud.
Mezzo Piano (*mp*)	Play moderately soft.
Moderato	Medium or moderate tempo.
Multiple Measure Rest	The number above the staff tells you how many full measures to rest. Count each measure of rest in sequence. (▬▬)
Music Staff	The Music Staff has 5 lines and 4 spaces where notes and rests are written.
Natural Sign (♮)	Cancels a flat (♭) or sharp (♯) and remains in effect for the entire measure.
Notes	Notes tell us how high or low to play by their placement on a line or space of the music staff, and how long to play by their shape.
Phrase	A Phrase is a musical "sentence," often 2 or 4 measures long.
Piano (*p*)	Play soft.
Pitch	The highness or lowness of a note which is indicated by the horizontal placement of the note on the music staff.
Pick-Up Notes	One or more notes that come before the first full measure. The beats of Pick-Up Notes are subtracted from the last measure.
Quarter Note	A Quarter Note (♩) receives one beat. There are 4 quarter notes in a $\frac{4}{4}$ measure.
Quarter Rest	The Quarter Rest (𝄽) marks one beat of silence.
Repeat Sign	The Repeat Sign (:‖) means to play once again from the beginning without pause. Repeat the section of music enclosed by the repeat signs (‖: :‖). If 1st and 2nd endings are used, they are played as usual—but go back only to the first repeat sign, not to the beginning.
Rests	Rests tell us to count silent beats.
Rhythm	Rhythm refers to how long, or for how many beats a note lasts.
Ritardando (*rit.*)	Means the tempo gradually gets slower.
Scale	A Scale is a sequence of notes in ascending or descending order. Like a musical "ladder," each step is the next consecutive note in the key signature.
Sharp (♯)	Raises the note a half step and remains in effect for the entire measure.

Glossary continued

Sixteenth Note	A sixteenth note ($\flat$ or $\flat$) has half the value of an eighth note. In $\frac{4}{4}$, $\frac{3}{4}$, or $\frac{2}{4}$ time, four sixteenth notes ($\sqcap\sqcap$) get one beat.
Slur	A curved line connecting notes of different pitch is called a Slur.
Staccato	Play the notes lightly and with separation.
Tempo	Tempo is the speed of music.
Tempo Markings	Tempo Markings are usually written above the staff, in Italian. (Allegro, Moderato, Andante)
Tenuto	Play the notes smoothly and connected, holding each note for its full value until the next is played.
Tie	A Tie is a curved line connecting two notes of the same pitch. It indicates that instead of playing both notes, you play the first note and hold it for the total time value of both notes.
Time Signature	Indicates how many beats per measure and what kind of note gets one beat.
Treble Clef ($\&$)	(G Clef) indicates the position of note names on a music staff: The second line in Treble Clef is G.
Trio	A Trio is a composition with three parts played together.
Triplet	A triplet is a group of three notes played in the time usually occupied by two. In $\frac{2}{4}$, $\frac{3}{4}$, or $\frac{4}{4}$ time, an eighth note triplet ($\sqcap\sqcap$) is spread evenly across one beat.
Whole Note	A Whole Note (o) lasts for four full beats (a complete measure in $\frac{4}{4}$ time).
Whole Rest	The Whole Rest (-) indicates a whole measure of silence.

Play Today! Series

The Ultimate Self-Teaching Series

These are complete guides to the basics, designed to offer quality instruction, terrific songs, and professional-quality audio with tons of full-demo tracks and instruction. Each book includes over 70 great songs and examples!

Play Accordion Today!
00701744	Level 1 Book/Audio	$10.99
00702657	Level 1 Songbook Book/Audio	$12.99

Play Alto Sax Today!
00842049	Level 1 Book/Audio	$9.99
00842050	Level 2 Book/Audio	$9.99
00320359	DVD	$14.95
00842051	Songbook Book/Audio	$12.95
00699555	Beginner's – Level 1 Book/Audio & DVD	$19.95
00699492	Play Today Plus Book/Audio	$14.95

Play Banjo Today!
00699897	Level 1 Book/Audio	$9.99
00701006	Level 2 Book/Audio	$9.99
00320913	DVD	$14.99
00115999	Songbook Book/Audio	$12.99
00701873	Beginner's – Level 1 Book/Audio & DVD	$19.95

Play Bass Today!
00842020	Level 1 Book/Audio	$9.99
00842036	Level 2 Book/Audio	$9.99
00320356	DVD	$14.95
00842037	Songbook Book/Audio	$12.95
00699552	Beginner's – Level 1 Book/Audio & DVD	$19.99

Play Cello Today!
00151353	Level 1 Book/Audio	$9.99

Play Clarinet Today!
00842046	Level 1 Book/Audio	$9.99
00842047	Level 2 Book/Audio	$9.99
00320358	DVD	$14.95
00842048	Songbook Book/Audio	$12.95
00699554	Beginner's – Level 1 Book/Audio & DVD	$19.95
00699490	Play Today Plus Book/Audio	$14.95

Play Dobro Today!
00701505	Level 1 Book/Audio	$9.99

Play Drums Today!
00842021	Level 1 Book/Audio	$9.99
00842038	Level 2 Book/Audio	$9.95
00320355	DVD	$14.95
00842039	Songbook Book/Audio	$12.95
00699551	Beginner's – Level 1 Book/Audio & DVD	$19.95
00703291	Starter	$24.99

Play Flute Today
00842043	Level 1 Book/Audio	$9.95
00842044	Level 2 Book/Audio	$9.99
00320360	DVD	$14.95
00842045	Songbook Book/Audio	$12.95
00699553	Beginner's – Level 1 Book/Audio & DVD	$19.95

Play Guitar Today!
00696100	Level 1 Book/Audio	$9.99
00696101	Level 2 Book/Audio	$9.99
00320353	DVD	$14.95
00696102	Songbook Book/Audio	$12.99
00699544	Beginner's – Level 1 Book/Audio & DVD	$19.95
00702431	Worship Songbook Book/Audio	$12.99
00695662	Complete Kit	$29.95

Play Harmonica Today!
00700179	Level 1 Book/Audio	$9.99
00320653	DVD	$14.99
00701875	Beginner's – Level 1 Book/Audio & DVD	$19.95

Play Mandolin Today!
00699911	Level 1 Book/Audio	$9.99
00320909	DVD	$14.99
00115029	Songbook Book/Audio	$12.99
00701874	Beginner's – Level 1 Book/Audio & DVD	$19.99

Play Piano Today!
Revised Edition
00842019	Level 1 Book/Audio	$9.99
00298773	Level 2 Book/Audio	$9.95
00842041	Songbook Book/Audio	$12.95
00699545	Beginner's – Level 1 Book/Audio & DVD	$19.95
00702415	Worship Songbook Book/Audio	$12.99
00703707	Complete Kit	$22.99

Play Recorder Today!
00700919	Level 1 Book/Audio	$7.99
00119830	Complete Kit	$19.99

Sing Today!
00699761	Level 1 Book/Audio	$10.99

Play Trombone Today!
00699917	Level 1 Book/Audio	$12.99
00320508	DVD	$14.95

Play Trumpet Today!
00842052	Level 1 Book/Audio	$9.99
00842053	Level 2 Book/Audio	$9.95
00320357	DVD	$14.95
00842054	Songbook Book/Audio	$12.95
00699556	Beginner's – Level 1 Book/Audio & DVD	$19.95

Play Ukulele Today!
00699638	Level 1 Book/Audio	$10.99
00699655	Play Today Plus Book/Audio	$9.99
00320985	DVD	$14.99
00701872	Beginner's – Level 1 Book/Audio & DVD	$19.95
00650743	Book/Audio/DVD with Ukulele	$39.99
00701002	Level 2 Book/Audio	$9.99
00702484	Level 2 Songbook Book/Audio	$12.99
00703290	Starter	$24.99

Play Viola Today!
00142679	Level 1 Book/Audio	$9.99

Play Violin Today!
00699748	Level 1 Book/Audio	$9.99
00701320	Level 2 Book/Audio	$9.99
00321076	DVD	$14.99
00701700	Songbook Book/Audio	$12.99
00701876	Beginner's – Level 1 Book/Audio & DVD	$19.95

HAL•LEONARD®

www.halleonard.com

HAL·LEONARD INSTRUMENTAL PLAY-ALONG

Your favorite songs are arranged just for solo instrumentalists with this outstanding series. Each book includes great full-accompaniment play-along audio so you can sound just like a pro!

Check out **halleonard.com** for songlists and more titles!

12 Pop Hits
12 songs

00261790	Flute	00261795	Horn
00261791	Clarinet	00261796	Trombone
00261792	Alto Sax	00261797	Violin
00261793	Tenor Sax	00261798	Viola
00261794	Trumpet	00261799	Cello

The Very Best of Bach
15 selections

00225371	Flute	00225376	Horn
00225372	Clarinet	00225377	Trombone
00225373	Alto Sax	00225378	Violin
00225374	Tenor Sax	00225379	Viola
00225375	Trumpet	00225380	Cello

The Beatles
15 songs

00225330	Flute	00225335	Horn
00225331	Clarinet	00225336	Trombone
00225332	Alto Sax	00225337	Violin
00225333	Tenor Sax	00225338	Viola
00225334	Trumpet	00225339	Cello

Chart Hits
12 songs

00146207	Flute	00146212	Horn
00146208	Clarinet	00146213	Trombone
00146209	Alto Sax	00146214	Violin
00146210	Tenor Sax	00146211	Trumpet
00146216	Cello		

Christmas Songs
12 songs

00146855	Flute	00146863	Horn
00146858	Clarinet	00146864	Trombone
00146859	Alto Sax	00146866	Violin
00146860	Tenor Sax	00146867	Viola
00146862	Trumpet	00146868	Cello

Contemporary Broadway
15 songs

00298704	Flute	00298709	Horn
00298705	Clarinet	00298710	Trombone
00298706	Alto Sax	00298711	Violin
00298707	Tenor Sax	00298712	Viola
00298708	Trumpet	00298713	Cello

Disney Movie Hits
12 songs

00841420	Flute	00841424	Horn
00841687	Oboe	00841425	Trombone
00841421	Clarinet	00841426	Violin
00841422	Alto Sax	00841427	Viola
00841686	Tenor Sax	00841428	Cello
00841423	Trumpet		

Prices, contents, and availability subject to change without notice.

Disney characters and artwork ™ & © 2021 Disney

Disney Solos
12 songs

00841404	Flute	00841506	Oboe
00841406	Alto Sax	00841409	Trumpet
00841407	Horn	00841410	Violin
00841411	Viola	00841412	Cello
00841405	Clarinet/Tenor Sax		
00841408	Trombone/Baritone		
00841553	Mallet Percussion		

Dixieland Favorites
15 songs

00268756	Flute	0068759	Trumpet
00268757	Clarinet	00268760	Trombone
00268758	Alto Sax		

Billie Eilish
9 songs

00345648	Flute	00345653	Horn
00345649	Clarinet	00345654	Trombone
00345650	Alto Sax	00345655	Violin
00345651	Tenor Sax	00345656	Viola
00345652	Trumpet	00345657	Cello

Favorite Movie Themes
13 songs

00841166	Flute	00841168	Trumpet
00841167	Clarinet	00841170	Trombone
00841169	Alto Sax	00841296	Violin

Gospel Hymns
15 songs

00194648	Flute	00194654	Trombone
00194649	Clarinet	00194655	Violin
00194650	Alto Sax	00194656	Viola
00194651	Tenor Sax	00194657	Cello
00194652	Trumpet		

Great Classical Themes
15 songs

00292727	Flute	00292733	Horn
00292728	Clarinet	00292735	Trombone
00292729	Alto Sax	00292736	Violin
00292730	Tenor Sax	00292737	Viola
00292732	Trumpet	00292738	Cello

The Greatest Showman
8 songs

00277389	Flute	00277394	Horn
00277390	Clarinet	00277395	Trombone
00277391	Alto Sax	00277396	Violin
00277392	Tenor Sax	00277397	Viola
00277393	Trumpet	00277398	Cello

Irish Favorites
31 songs

00842489	Flute	00842495	Trombone
00842490	Clarinet	00842496	Violin
00842491	Alto Sax	00842497	Viola
00842493	Trumpet	00842498	Cello
00842494	Horn		

Michael Jackson
11 songs

00119495	Flute	00119499	Trumpet
00119496	Clarinet	00119501	Trombone
00119497	Alto Sax	00119503	Violin
00119498	Tenor Sax	00119502	Accomp.

Jazz & Blues
14 songs

00841438	Flute	00841441	Trumpet
00841439	Clarinet	00841443	Trombone
00841440	Alto Sax	00841444	Violin
00841442	Tenor Sax		

Jazz Classics
12 songs

00151812	Flute	00151816	Trumpet
00151813	Clarinet	00151818	Trombone
00151814	Alto Sax	00151819	Violin
00151815	Tenor Sax	00151821	Cello

Les Misérables
13 songs

00842292	Flute	00842297	Horn
00842293	Clarinet	00842298	Trombone
00842294	Alto Sax	00842299	Violin
00842295	Tenor Sax	00842300	Viola
00842296	Trumpet	00842301	Cello

Metallica
12 songs

02501327	Flute	02502454	Horn
02501339	Clarinet	02501329	Trombone
02501332	Alto Sax	02501334	Violin
02501333	Tenor Sax	02501335	Viola
02501330	Trumpet	02501338	Cello

Motown Classics
15 songs

00842572	Flute	00842576	Trumpet
00842573	Clarinet	00842578	Trombone
00842574	Alto Sax	00842579	Violin
00842575	Tenor Sax		

Pirates of the Caribbean
16 songs

00842183	Flute	00842188	Horn
00842184	Clarinet	00842189	Trombone
00842185	Alto Sax	00842190	Violin
00842186	Tenor Sax	00842191	Viola
00842187	Trumpet	00842192	Cello

Queen
17 songs

00285402	Flute	00285407	Horn
00285403	Clarinet	00285408	Trombone
00285404	Alto Sax	00285409	Violin
00285405	Tenor Sax	00285410	Viola
00285406	Trumpet	00285411	Cello

Simple Songs
14 songs

00249081	Flute	00249087	Horn
00249093	Oboe	00249089	Trombone
00249082	Clarinet	00249090	Violin
00249083	Alto Sax	00249091	Viola
00249084	Tenor Sax	00249092	Cello
00249086	Trumpet	00249094	Mallets

Superhero Themes
14 songs

00363195	Flute	00363200	Horn
00363196	Clarinet	00363201	Trombone
00363197	Alto Sax	00363202	Violin
00363198	Tenor Sax	00363203	Viola
00363199	Trumpet	00363204	Cello

Star Wars
16 songs

00350900	Flute	00350907	Horn
00350913	Oboe	00350908	Trombone
00350903	Clarinet	00350909	Violin
00350904	Alto Sax	00350910	Viola
00350905	Tenor Sax	00350911	Cello
00350906	Trumpet	00350914	Mallet

Taylor Swift
15 songs

00842532	Flute	00842537	Horn
00842533	Clarinet	00842538	Trombone
00842534	Alto Sax	00842539	Violin
00842535	Tenor Sax	00842540	Viola
00842536	Trumpet	00842541	Cello

Video Game Music
13 songs

00283877	Flute	00283883	Horn
00283878	Clarinet	00283884	Trombone
00283879	Alto Sax	00283885	Violin
00283880	Tenor Sax	00283886	Viola
00283882	Trumpet	00283887	Cello

Wicked
13 songs

00842236	Flute	00842241	Horn
00842237	Clarinet	00842242	Trombone
00842238	Alto Sax	00842243	Violin
00842239	Tenor Sax	00842244	Viola
00842240	Trumpet	00842245	Cello

HAL·LEONARD®

101 SONGS

BIG COLLECTIONS OF FAVORITE SONGS ARRANGED FOR SOLO INSTRUMENTALISTS.

101 BROADWAY SONGS

00154199	Flute	$15.99
00154200	Clarinet	$15.99
00154201	Alto Sax	$15.99
00154202	Tenor Sax	$16.99
00154203	Trumpet	$15.99
00154204	Horn	$15.99
00154205	Trombone	$15.99
00154206	Violin	$15.99
00154207	Viola	$15.99
00154208	Cello	$15.99

101 DISNEY SONGS

00244104	Flute	$17.99
00244106	Clarinet	$17.99
00244107	Alto Sax	$17.99
00244108	Tenor Sax	$17.99
00244109	Trumpet	$17.99
00244112	Horn	$17.99
00244120	Trombone	$17.99
00244121	Violin	$17.99
00244125	Viola	$17.99
00244126	Cello	$17.99

101 MOVIE HITS

00158087	Flute	$15.99
00158088	Clarinet	$15.99
00158089	Alto Sax	$15.99
00158090	Tenor Sax	$15.99
00158091	Trumpet	$15.99
00158092	Horn	$15.99
00158093	Trombone	$15.99
00158094	Violin	$15.99
00158095	Viola	$15.99
00158096	Cello	$15.99

101 CHRISTMAS SONGS

00278637	Flute	$15.99
00278638	Clarinet	$15.99
00278639	Alto Sax	$15.99
00278640	Tenor Sax	$15.99
00278641	Trumpet	$15.99
00278642	Horn	$14.99
00278643	Trombone	$15.99
00278644	Violin	$15.99
00278645	Viola	$15.99
00278646	Cello	$15.99

101 HIT SONGS

00194561	Flute	$17.99
00197182	Clarinet	$17.99
00197183	Alto Sax	$17.99
00197184	Tenor Sax	$17.99
00197185	Trumpet	$17.99
00197186	Horn	$17.99
00197187	Trombone	$17.99
00197188	Violin	$17.99
00197189	Viola	$17.99
00197190	Cello	$17.99

101 POPULAR SONGS

00224722	Flute	$17.99
00224723	Clarinet	$17.99
00224724	Alto Sax	$17.99
00224725	Tenor Sax	$17.99
00224726	Trumpet	$17.99
00224727	Horn	$17.99
00224728	Trombone	$17.99
00224729	Violin	$17.99
00224730	Viola	$17.99
00224731	Cello	$17.99

101 CLASSICAL THEMES

00155315	Flute	$15.99
00155317	Clarinet	$15.99
00155318	Alto Sax	$15.99
00155319	Tenor Sax	$15.99
00155320	Trumpet	$15.99
00155321	Horn	$15.99
00155322	Trombone	$15.99
00155323	Violin	$15.99
00155324	Viola	$15.99
00155325	Cello	$15.99

101 JAZZ SONGS

00146363	Flute	$15.99
00146364	Clarinet	$15.99
00146366	Alto Sax	$15.99
00146367	Tenor Sax	$15.99
00146368	Trumpet	$15.99
00146369	Horn	$14.99
00146370	Trombone	$15.99
00146371	Violin	$15.99
00146372	Viola	$15.99
00146373	Cello	$15.99

101 MOST BEAUTIFUL SONGS

00291023	Flute	$16.99
00291041	Clarinet	$16.99
00291042	Alto Sax	$17.99
00291043	Tenor Sax	$17.99
00291044	Trumpet	$16.99
00291045	Horn	$16.99
00291046	Trombone	$16.99
00291047	Violin	$16.99
00291048	Viola	$16.99
00291049	Cello	$17.99

See complete song lists and sample pages at www.halleonard.com

HAL•LEONARD®
www.halleonard.com

Prices, contents and availability subject to change without notice.

EXCEPTIONAL FLUTE PUBLICATIONS from HAL LEONARD

BIG BOOK OF FLUTE SONGS
Flutists will love this giant collection of 130 popular solos! Includes: Another One Bites the Dust • Any Dream Will Do • Bad Day • Beauty and the Beast • Breaking Free • Clocks • Edelweiss • God Bless the U.S.A. • Heart and Soul • I Will Remember You • Imagine • Na Na Hey Hey Kiss Him Goodbye • Satin Doll • United We Stand • You Raise Me Up • and dozens more!
00842207 $14.95

CLAUDE BOLLING – SUITE FOR FLUTE AND JAZZ PIANO TRIO
This suite in seven parts is composed for a "classic" flute and a "jazz" piano. It was the first jazz recording of world-renowned flutist Jean-Pierre Rampal and Claude Bolling. It is possible to play the whole piece with only flute and piano, but bass and drum parts are included for the complete Suite. The CD includes full recordings and flute play-along tracks for seven songs: Baroque and Blue • Fugace • Irlandaise • Javanaise • Sentimentale • Veloce • Versatile.
00672558   Set of Parts/CD $59.95

THE BOOSEY & HAWKES FLUTE ANTHOLOGY
24 PIECES BY 16 COMPOSERS
Boosey & Hawkes
Intermediate to advanced literature from the Romantic era to the 20th century. Special study paid to various state high school contest solo repertory lists. Contents: Gavotte and Musette from Divertimento (Alwyn) • Scherzo from Suite Paysanne Hongroise (Bartók) • First Movement from Duo for Flute and Piano (Copland) • Vocalise (Copland) • Valentine Piece, Op. 70 (Górecki) • Duo for Two Flutes (Lees) • Rhapsody on a Theme of Paganini, Op. 43 (Rachmaninoff) • and many more.
48019634 $24.99

ÉTUDES MODERNES POUR FLUTE
[MODERN STUDIES FOR FLUTE]
Alphonse Leduc
Modern Studies for the Flute is a set of sixteen studies by Paul Jeanjean (1874-1928). Composed in 1868, and initially composed for clarinet, these studies would fit advanced players. Each one of these *Modern Studies* is 3 or 4 pages long and extremely technically challenging.
48182950 $39.99

FLUTE FINGERING CHART
FOR FLUTE AND PICCOLO
In addition to a detailed fingering chart, this handy laminated fold-out card includes notes about instrument care, transposition, pitch system, and notation. A valuable tool for any flute player!
14011341 $7.95

THE G. SCHIRMER FLUTE ANTHOLOGY
14 WORKS FROM THE 20TH CENTURY
G. Schirmer, Inc.
Selected works from the most prominent G. Schirmer and AMP composers, including music by Barber, Corigliano, Harbison, Martinu, Moyse, Muczynski, and others. With detailed notes on the music. Suitable for the advanced high school and college level player. Includes works for solo flute as well as flute and piano.
50499531 $19.99

IMPROVISATION FOR FLUTE
THE SCALE/MODE APPROACH
by Andy McGhee
Berklee Press
Expand the creative breadth of your soloing! The step-by-step exercises and explanations in this tried-&-true resource will help you develop your ear and improve your technique. You'll learn the intimate relationships between modes and chords, practicing licks and solos that grow out of their underlying harmonies and sound natural.
50449810 $16.99

JAZZ FLUTE ETUDES
Houston Publishing, Inc.
These etudes by Marc Adler will delight both classical and jazz musicians. Marc is an accomplished flutist and composer in both the jazz and classical arenas and is also an experienced educator. These twelve etudes explore each of the twelve keys but at the same time step out into contemporary sounds characteristic of modern jazz and 20th-century classical music, such as whole tone and diminished scales, and colorful chord progressions. Jazz flutists will enjoy his original jazz licks and may want to add some of them to their vocabulary of patterns.
00030442 $14.99

JETHRO TULL – FLUTE SOLOS
AS PERFORMED BY IAN ANDERSON
transcribed by Jeff Rona
Flute solos from 18 Jethro Tull songs have been transcribed for this collection. Songs include: Bungle in the Jungle • Cross-Eyed Mary • Fire at Midnight • Look into the Sun • Nothing Is Easy • Thick as a Brick • The Witch's Promise • and more.
00672547 $15.99

101 FLUTE TIPS
STUFF ALL THE PROS KNOW AND USE
by Elaine Schmidt
Tips, suggestions, advice and other useful information garnered through a lifetime of flute study and professional gigging are all presented in this book with dozens of entries gleaned from first-hand experience. Topics covered include: selecting the right flute for you • finding the right teacher • warm-up exercises • practicing effectively • taking good care of your flute • gigging advice • staying and playing healthy • members of the flute family • extended ranges and techniques • and flute fraternization.
00119883   Book/CD Pack $14.99